# Coffee Sh ... Smart Startup

# How to Start, Run & Grow a Trendy Coffee House on a Budget

## By

# Rick Robinson

Published by:

**Valley Of Joy Publishing Press**

Cover & Interior designed

By

Rebecca Floyd

*First Edition*

# What is Covered Here

**************************************************

# INTRODUCTION TO COFFEE HOUSE BUSINESS

Driving around the city in any metropolitan areas we all see trendy coffee shops everywhere and not all of them are Starbucks. Do you ever wonder why there are so many new boutique coffee shops popping up everywhere? Well, according to

National Coffee Association (http://www.ncausa.org), it is not a hoax, but the new trend and this is the reality. The coffee industry and the coffee shop business has boomed in recent years, especially with regards to specialty coffees. The market for specialty coffees has grown as consumers become more educated about espresso-based drinks and how they are made.

_Here is what CCAUSA has gathered from their research:_

- Out of home coffee consumption has reached a new high of 46% in 2017
- 59% of coffee consumed daily are gourmet coffee
- In the US more than 65% adult population drink coffee every day that means roughly about 70 million daily coffee drinkers.
- 66% of people in the US buy their daily coffee outside their home
- Gross profit margin for most coffee shops are around 85%
- In US coffee shop business is a 10 billion dollar industry.

Let these number sink in for a minute. Let's agree that all these numbers are saying one thing that is the coffee industry has been on the rise for last few years, and it will continue to grow. The best part is once you become a coffee drinker, you are a coffee drinker for life. Since the growth is mostly coming from the young adult population that also means this is the new trendy thing to do among that segment of the population. Honestly, they are usually the best customers to have.

Okay, now that we established the fact that coffee is growing the industry and investing in it is not a bad idea. Let's talk about how to get into this business when resources are limited. I opened my first coffee shop in 2013 for $37000. Before you ask how I was able to do that with such a low investment. I will tell you that the storefront we found and rented was a sandwich shop before.

So we didn't have to do any plumbing, electrical, HVAC work which saved us a lot of money. The store even had a walk-in cooler. Our funds were spent on equipment, store decoration, furniture, lighting, signs and new wood flooring. Sometimes if you look hard enough, you should be able to find something similar where you may not have to do a lot of construction work.

If you are thinking about opening a coffee house, here are the 13 steps that you will need to take:

- Funding, depending on where you are and what you may find available for lease, it will be safe to assume that you will need in between $35,000 - $185,000 to one of these up and running. If you think the range is too broad, it is, because prices vary widely based on your geographic location.

- Business Plan. A well thought out business plan is a must-have. This is the blueprint you will follow to your ultimate success.

- Site selection and lease.   Finding the right location is the key to your success. You want to be in an area where there is foot traffic and or around office parks or even around a mid-sized strip mall. You can also pick a storefront next to a major road or highway where you are visible from both direction, but for this type locations, you will have to have a drive-thru to survive.

various food vendors and trying out various samples and discussing prices.

- Pricing Your Products. This is where you set up menu prices, set up your POS and implement proper training, so there is no mistake made when ringing up a customer.

- Soft & Grand Opening. Once you feel that everything is done, ready and set to go, go ahead and do a soft opening before you advertise and do a grand opening. This way you get all the kinks out before doing the grand opening.

- Marketing and Promotion.

If you are ready, let's get started, let's see how we can put you in the driver's seat of a very successful trendy coffee shop that you can be proud of.

# MONEY, MONEY, MONEY.
## ALWAYS SUNNY

Remember the famous Abba song, "Money, money, money"? Well, that is what you will need first to get started on your dream project.

There are few ways to go about finding the required funds.

1. Your own savings/401K etc.
2. Home equity line of credit (this is how I got started with mine)

3. Family funding (where your parents, siblings help you with a personal loan)
4. Create partnership with people that have the money
5. Crowdfunding
6. Applying for a small business loan at your local bank

Sit down, take a piece of paper, try to analyze each and every option and then see which one seems more doable for you. You can even do a mix and match here. For example, you need $100,000 to open your coffee shop, but you only have $50,000, one idea is to ask one or two like-minded friends or family to come in as a 50% partner, where you hold 50% of the business, the other two gets 25% each.

As for crowdfunding, I have never done it, but have seen people do it. You can make a list of 10-20 people that you know. Ask each of them for an investment of $10,000 for a 7% stake in your company. If 10 of them agree, you will have $100,000, and you only gave out 70% of your business. The remaining 30% is still yours for FREE.

You just have to be creative, remember when there is a strong will power to achieve something, there is always a way to get there.

As for applying for a loan at the bank is the hardest of all other methods I outlined above. In the event you have no other option but to apply for a loan, you do have to do some research first.

First come up with a list of banks you want to apply to, it is not a good idea to apply at multiple banks at once, instead come up with a list of say four banks. Visit of them and talk in depth with their business loan department and find out if that bank offers loans for your type of projects, there are banks that do not offer loans for restaurants.

In my experience, I have noticed typically smaller local banks are more inclined to offer loans to local family-owned restaurants, coffee shops, and another similar type of businesses than some of the bigger banks. But that may not be true for every part of the country, so it is best to talk to at least 3-4 banks and try to get the feel if they are really into these sort of business financing or not before you submit your application.

Sometimes your local business brokers or commercial real estate agents can guide you to the right bank as they often deal with similar situations and knows which banks are more favorable to these sort of loans. You can also ask your bank that you deal with every day and ask for their advice.

Now once you narrow down to say two banks, visit them, have a meeting with their loan officer and see what their requirements are. Just remember every bank will have similar requirements, but still, they can vary widely based on many factors like how much down payment they require, how much collateral they will need from you to even if they offer some SBA assisted loans or not. Your goal would be to deal with a bank that offers SBA loan, SBA stands for Small Business Administration. This is where federal government guarantees part of your loan to the bank.

Most times SBA offers some sort of guarantee(typically 50-80%) on your behalf to the bank, so banks are somewhat more lenient in approving the loan as they are not in the risk for the total amount they are giving you. But the downside to this is the amount of paperwork you have to furnish is monumental in most cases.

SBA's requirements can be broad and extensive, so be prepared to gather up a lot of paperwork.

Another drawback to SBA loan is it can take up to 4 months to get approval from them as they run slower than most banks and in their defense, they do have a lot of applicants that are submitting applications. Which they have to go through all them, it is always first come first serve, so be patient.

But if you have larger down payment (30% or higher) or have some good collateral to offer, then you can opt out on SBA loans and get most any banks to provide you a conventional business loan. Provided you have all your ducks in a row like your credit is in excellent shape, your tax returns show good incomes for previous years and so on so forth.

When you talk to any banks, they will hand you something call a loan package, most times the package will have a checklist of documents that you need to furnish to them along with a loan application and some other waiver forms depending on your bank.

One thing to keep in mind, all banks and commercial lenders do have to follow certain guideline that is set by federal and state banking authorities. Also, every bank will look at something call LTV (Loan to Value) ratio of the property or business you are looking to buy. LTV is essentially where banks look at the actual value of the business you are looking to buy or lease and how much of that value they can loan you.

Let's look at the list of documents you will need to get ready to submit to your bank. Some of these items I will mention here may not be on your bank's checklist but do gather them anyway as it will make you look more professional and business-like.

## Here is What You Need to Gather:

1. You need to get copies of at least last three years of personal tax returns, make sure the copies are signed.

2. Your resume (they may not even ask you for it, but remember the person that may approve your loan may never meet you but this way at least he or she gets to see who you are and how qualified you are it always helps)

3. Copy of your Corp. Articles, (yes you have to get this done before you even apply for your loan, I will touch on how to file a corporation in the next chapter)

4. Personal financial statement for all Corp. Officers or members, make sure to sign it, if you are married and file joint tax returns than your wife needs to have one prepared for her as well or you can make a joint personal financial statement for both of you and make sure to both sign that document.

5. Copy of the commercial appraisal (in the event you are buying a location instead of leasing)

6. Copy of signed purchase agreement and Letter of intent (in the event you are buying)

7. Copy of your EIN (Employer's Identification Number) issued by the IRS

8. Copy of all member/partner's Driver's licenses and social security cards

9. A well thought out and expertly written Business Plan (not a store bought one or copy-pasted one, one that is written for your specific business, get help if you need to, but this has to be a well thought out plan, do it like your life depends on it trust me on this.)

10. Last but the least the loan application all filled out, use a computer and printer if possible, if not write very clearly, so it is easy to read.

11. A cover letter addressed to the loan department where you describe what is in the package and thanking them for reviewing your loan application and lastly tell them where they easily reach you if they need further help or other documents from you, it just makes you look more professional.

Now, remember to organize these papers with nice tabs and in a binding folder where anyone can open the folder, looking at the tabs, they can go directly to that specific section.

If you are applying for an SBA specific business loan then SBA may also give you a loan package with some more documents and forms to fill out, but they will mostly ask for the same as I just mentioned. But yes they will have you fill out many more forms, and don't worry you do not have to visit SBA office separately they work through your local banks so the loan officer you deal with will furnish you all of that.

# BUSINESS PLAN

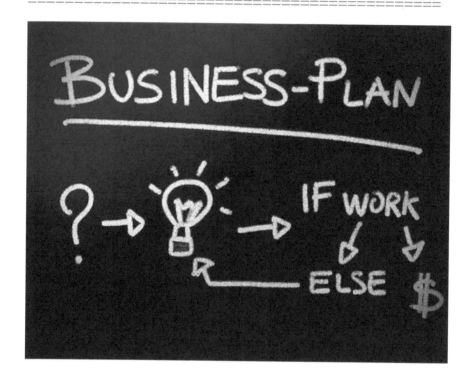

When thinking about opening a coffee shop, you will need to consider many things, but making sure that you have a solid business plan is essential. A great way to ensure that you do not miss any actions necessary to the successful opening of your coffee shop is to write a business plan for your coffee shop.

There are many reasons why many current and future coffee shop owners might think that a business plan isn't always warranted.

# 5 BIGGEST MISCONCEPTIONS ABOUT BUSINESS PLAN

## *No one ever told them about a business plan before*

It's natural that many coffee shop owners maybe wouldn't have been exposed to the process of creating a business plan. While some businesses can succeed without one, it is not the suggested method of opening a business. The first thing you may want to familiarize yourself with the different points the business plan will highlight.

## *They are confused on where to start*

So, a business owner may know think they need a business plan, but just may not understand where they need to start and so, they just decided not to do it. This is not ever a good idea. Every business owner has to begin at some point. You have to find a way to begin your business plan if you want to be able to use it to bring your dreams to life.

### They think it is just too hard

Starting a business plan doesn't have to be difficult, but you have to put the work in. It also takes a large amount of thoughtfulness and time. While planning doesn't always guarantee success, not planning will almost definitely lead to failure. It may not seem like a fun thing to do, losing all of your money in a terrible business doesn't seem too fun either. To start your plan, you don't have to start from scratch. There are many online resources to get you started.

### They think their business is too small to be worth the trouble

You might think that a business plan would be overkill because you are just starting one small business but, even for small business would benefit from having a business plan thoughtfully written. Even small businesses have hundreds of things to keep track of and consider.

### You think you can keep all the plans in their head

Sometimes business owners think that they should rely on their mental abilities or just their memories instead of taking the time to develop their business plan. But they are not considering when starting a business; you will be way too busy working on the day-to-day operations to remember everything that you would need to do to open your business.

## WHY YOU NEED A BUSINESS PLAN FOR YOUR COFFEE SHOP

### YOUR BUSINESS PLAN WILL SAVE YOU MONEY

No matter how much you love the different beans, flavors, and tools related to making coffee, it is important to remember that a coffee shop is a business. Without having organizational chart and estimate on profitability, your business will not succeed. So, plan as much as possible in the beginning.

When you start any kind of business, it is almost impossible not to go beyond the original budget estimates. Underestimating the expenses for a coffee shop so typical, even if you have a well formatted and thought- out business plan.

A way to avoid overspending and sticker shock is to anticipate your expenses accurately, then add 5 to 10 percent to that. Use this number as if you don't have a penny more. Don't buy what you don't need and can't afford. A business plan is a perfect place to have a written-out plan of expenses. Also, if you have a business plan, it will help you consider the basic financial costs that anyone can easily overlook.

With this information, you should realize that If you do not have a written-out plan, you will more than likely spend much more money and waste a considerably larger amount of time because you have planned no way to manage the budget for your coffee shop effectively.

## YOUR BUSINESS PLAN WILL KEEP YOU ORGANIZED

Being organized saves every business money. This habit also saves business owners stress and headaches. A business plan can start your coffee shop off on the right foot. After creating a business plan, you would them know the pace of which things need to be started and completed what tasked have yet to be finished. However, with so much to think over, writing them all down might not be the best use of your time.

You can use your business plan as a general checklist. You have to be somewhat general, without all of the small details involved with completing your tasks. Choosing not to include too many details is important because you want your business plan to stay at a readable length. You want just enough information so that you and other people can read and understand the plan.

## YOUR BUSINESS PLAN WILL KEEP YOU ON TRACK

It doesn't matter if you have needed one or a hundred businesses, there are always specific elements that you have to address it the initial steps in starting up your coffee shop business. If you recently forget things you will have to work backward, wasting money and time. So having a business plan will keep you on track, making sure that no tasks are left undone.

Remember that your business plan will be read by Investors, banks, and stakeholders as well as your property manager

With all writing, considering your audience is very important. The document needs to be tailored to their requirements as well as your own. The audience for your business plan is pretty small but very important. Your property manager will most likely want to see a business plan from you to make sure that you plan for their space will be beneficial to them as wells practical.

You could not know it, but they might actually have had a few different competing business proposals for their properties. Your business plan will need to be a well thought out and articulate description of your vision and goals.

Because they are investing their money in you and your business, they want to assess their risk. Stakeholders and potential investors will want a well thought out business plan before choosing to invest.

## YOUR BUSINESS PLAN WILL HELP YOU ANSWER 4 IMPORTANT QUESTIONS

There will be quite a few important questions that will need to be answered in the planning phase of your coffee shop. A huge element of the planning phase would be will spending considerable time figuring your budget and spending. As spoken about previously, the financial projections are a large hurdle to get over.

Know that just because it is difficult doesn't mean that you can avoid the tasks, just doing a general overview, and not do anything at all is one of the worst things you can do for your fledgling business. Start a habit of keeping excellent financial records and staying close to your budget at all times. This is important, especially in the beginning.

## ISN'T WRITING A BUSINESS PLAN DIFFICULT?

Writing a business plan certainly doesn't have to be hard. It is crucial to follow along with the process as close to as possible. Simplicity is the key. You have goals and dreams for your business, so your business plan turns all of those goals and dreams into an actual business. A real-life entity that you run. This is the first step to taking your goals and making them into a reality. Your business plan can be a written guideline for you to be able to follow well past opening day. This will keep you close to your original goals and vision.

It really is up to you how complex your business plan is. It is important to remember that you want to be able to come back to this document over and over again. This can end up wasting a lot of time if you have an unnecessarily lengthy document. You will avoid it instead of using it as the resource as it is. A complex document will not impress anyone.

It will also take some time to think through as well as solve the potential problems that can arise when writing your business plan. The most important thing to remember is to remain positive and approach the task in a cool and calm manner.

You don't have to write your entire business plan in one afternoon. In fact, don't even try. Spend time brainstorming. Think about what exactly what you want and then plan the exact way that you will be able to achieve these goals.

Start with your overall goals. Then break each goal into one to three smaller goals and then go from theirs. Choose to see it as an opportunity for you to get those creative juices flowing. It's fun to really figure out the wants and needs of your potential business.

The more positively you look at the process, the more likely it will be that you finish with a document that you both feel it a representative of your future business and yourself.

## How Long Does a Business Plan Have to Be?

This is a kind of tough question to answer. The reason for this that is that the time length really depends on the individual and the individual business, and the complexity of the chosen concept. A good ballpark for a coffee shop business plan should be anywhere from 1- to 15 pages once it's completed.

It can be even more depending on your needs for details. It might sound like it's a lot, but in reality, it's not. You should always use Headings as well as subheadings. Also, space between paragraphs and sections are important for readability when constructing your business plan. This will also give you a place to write notes in the margins.

Here is a website that you can check out, they prepare custom business plans for various businesses once you provide them with enough data. I have used them before, and I can say they do a great job.

http://BPlans.com

## WHAT'S INSIDE A BUSINESS PLAN?

A business plan has five to seven main sections that absolutely have to be addressed. Know that there is no perfect structure for a business plan. You do need to have some standard things included. Business plans will typically mention your mission statement in the beginning sections and include important elements such as the equipment you will need as well as your financial position with budget estimates.

Also, there isn't any kind of standard order that your business plan has to come in, it just needs to follow a logical sequence. I will give you a mini example of a business plan and what elements can be considered for inclusion below.

# Should I Just Pay Someone to Write My Coffee Shop Business Plan for Me?

It may seem like having someone write your business plan would be a great idea. You may not like to write, or may not want to do the research on creating a business plan. It is possible to have someone write your business plan. But a site like boplans.com has enough expertise to create a better plan then what you most likely will be able to create all on your own.

Actually writing your business plan can really give you a sense of ownership in your business. It is your coffee shop; it should be your plan.

# Creating a Budget for Now and the Future

| Startup Expenses | |
|---|---|
| Furniture | $15,500.00 |
| Décor | $12,700.00 |
| Designing | $7,500.00 |
| Construction & Layout | $22,500.00 |
| Menu and POS | $8,000.00 |
| Equipment | $23,000.00 |
| Rent and Insurance | $4,500.00 |
| Legal and Licenses | $2,500.00 |
| Stationnery and Uniform | $1,800.00 |
| Startup Cash | $5,000.00 |
| Startup Inventory | $5,000.00 |
| **Total Startup Expenses** | **$108,000.00** |

If you have dreamed of opening your very own coffee shop, you have probably thought about some concepts in your head about the kind of coffee shop you'd want to have. Settling on just one concept can take time. And it very well should, since your coffee shop concept will impact your startup costs and future costs considerably.

Whether you want a small coffee stand or a large coffee shop with a bookstore, both the initial startup costs and the everyday operational costs will be very different. Remember, as you learn more about the coffee business, your business plan or concept may need to change. This is just fine. It happens all the time. This makes perfect sense because as your depth of your understanding grows deeper, your concept will have to change naturally.

It is important to know what your budget is like and what it will be like in the future. Then you need to figure out the profit level you will need to break-even.

The first step to knowing if you can afford a coffee shop is to figure out what your specific kind of shop will cost and then figure out how much money do you have access to start your coffee shop is the next step.

When determining how much money it will take to open a coffee shop, you have to consider a variety of variables that go into the type of business you want. So for example, you might have $20,000 in a savings account and, you know that you can borrow another $8,000 from your family. You now know how much money you have access to.

It is important to be completely honest with yourself when it comes to both the money you actually have and the money you would have access to. This will help you figure out just how much you would need to rise to create the business you want.

Your break-even point is an important number to figure out. It will help you to determine your profitability. First, you will need to add up all of the startup costs and the everyday costs and determine how much you will need to break-even

Remember to leave room for flexibility. As you begin to develop your concept, your budget and will begin to change naturally. This usually means that you will eventually end up needing more money than you thought in the beginning.

Also, it means that your money will need to be reshuffled, giving more to one aspect while taking away from another, don't ever be afraid to adjust your budget when needed.

No matter what change comes along, be sure to update your business plan to be in line with any those changes accordingly. As I mentioned previously while it is important to create a plan, there is no need to overcomplicate your budget. Simplicity is always the best way.

## SAMPLE OF A BUSINESS PLAN

### Table of Contents

## II   Background

The operating plan is for the new site in the heart of Downtown Birmingham for a new CoffeeBuddie (The Store). This development is one of the newest shopping sites in the area and already has anchor tenants such as Barnes and Noble, J C penny and few other big-name retail outlets. The growth of downtown Birmingham in last five years has been phenomenal, and there is no CoffeeBuddie in the area, and it will be a first in the area.

## III   Planning of the New Store

The proposed CoffeeBuddie will be a 1440 SQF in size inside store seating occupancy is about 65 people, outside seating is 12 and the operation hours will be from 10:00 am until 9:00 pm for the convenience of the guests.

## IV   Management Team

CoffeeBuddie LLC is an Alabama corporation. It has two members; Jack Ross, the president of this entity, owns 50% share of the company. Mr. Ross has extensive experience in operating, managing and owning various QSR type restaurants in the local area for last 17 years. John Smith is the other member who holds 50% share of the company. He has 20 years of solid experience in running, managing and operating Burger King, Quiznos, and a trendy Ice Cream shop in town.

## V     Reason for Choosing CoffeeBuddie

CoffeeBuddie LLC. Recognizes that Gourmet coffee and cakes are in high demand and the growth of such coffee shops are on the rise. CoffeeBuddie is already made a good name in its other location when it comes to quality and delicious coffee and bakery offerings. CoffeeBuddie has consistently provided good quality food and coffee prepared with the freshest ingredients.

## VI     Target Market

The store is surrounded by big office buildings as it is in the heart of Birmingham Downtown. There are few residential apartments and single-family homes also. Store's target customers would be the employees of the courthouse, city hall and all the banks and other offices, business, medical offices, local residents and the community and the people driving on the nearby roads and highways.

## VII     Competition

Following are the direct and indirect competitors:

- Starbucks
- Java Jolt

Since CoffeeBuddie has unique coffee and bakery offerings with its patented and tasty flavor, the existence of direct and indirect competition will have a very minimal impact on the sales and revenues of the store.

## VIII     Long-Term Goals

John Smith will be running the day-to-day operations. He strongly believes that just by utilizing his own past experience & talents in operating retail operation such as this, he will be able to make progress in saving labor & other costs that will bring the bottom line. Mr. Smith is also very positive about creating a campaign to advertise & market the CoffeeBuddie with the local neighborhood, especially increasing the customer service and creating a positive professional relationship with the customers by mingling with them in a daily basis. CoffeeBuddie LLC has the vision of opening multiple CoffeeBuddie locations within next three years, eventually be a successful owner, operator for multiple profitable Stores.

## IX    Financial Sources

Mr. Ross is financially strong, has an excellent credit history, and meets the net worth and liquidity requirements set by CoffeeBuddie. The loan has been obtained from Finley bank.

## X    operational Issues

Mr. Smith will manage the Store, with the assistance of the following staff:

| TITLE | NUMBER |
|---|---|
| Store Manager / Owner | 1 |
| Assistant Manager | 1 |
| Associates | 10 |

Mr. Smith will be in charge of all employee and management training and support.

# XI    Professional Support

Liberty Group LLC has the following consultant / professional that will help in the initial stages of taking over the store and on an ongoing basis after the takeover:

- Mike Smith
  Attorney at Law

  Alexander & Associates.

  2501 First Avenue

  Birmingham, Al 33401


- James Foster CPA
  5920 Omni Professional Park

  Hoover, Al 33212

-----------------------------------------------------------------------

# LOCATION, LOCATION, LOCATION

(Credit – Isainsider.com)

When deciding on the best location for your business, think about the successful coffee shops you already know and frequent yourself. The location of your store is an important factor when considering your property.

Location is often what will make or break a business, you could be the best Barista in the world, yet if your store location is in an area of town that lacks foot traffic, parking, or has a tattoo shop right next door that has people hanging around it all day, it might not be the best place to set up a space for your customers to come and relax. The best locations are close to strip malls, office complexes or even on a corner of a busy roadway. Again, look at where other successful Coffee operators are positioned, and this will help you to formulate your own plant on your location hunt.

Your research is critical, come up with the area you want your shop to be, visit the area, and look up the local demographics. Is it a seasonal area? Are there any festivals, or major events that happen in this area?  Will you get more foot traffic through certain times of the year, or will you get a steady flow of customers all year round? Do you want only a take away facility, or would you prefer a sit-down area for your customers to enjoy their coffee? These are critical factors in deciding where your location will best suit your own personal vision.

Think outside of the square, your location may not initially look like a coffee shop that you are used to. It may have a particular "vibe", something that will attract a certain clientele that you can build on. Once, people would go to pubs and bars to watch sports, although drinking at a bar is not everyone's "cup of coffee". Around the world, coffee bars that have large screen televisions, unique blends of furniture, comfortable lounges and coffee tables for groups to sit at, and even book shelves full of second hand books to enjoy while drinking coffee. These spaces are individual, and unique which offers you an edge.

I once saw a warehouse, within walking distance to the local business center, converted into a coffee house. It was full of old and rustic chairs and wooden tables. What made it unique is it attracted local artists, who would arrive with their blank canvasses and ask for shot glasses with different strength coffee in them. They then proceeded to paint using coffee as the medium.

This project became a source of interest to the public and the artists would have spectators, who bought coffee, drank coffee, and watched the artists create their masterpiece. The art work was often on sale through the store. As you can see, as a concept for thinking about what you want to achieve is only limited to your imagination.

Another hugely popular option for a coffee vendor is not to have a store location at all, have a Coffee van! Coffee vans give you the freedom to travel with your business, work your own hours and choose your locations. Vans are successful for Markets, Festivals, Functions, and Beaches on the weekend, sporting events, and the list is endless.

You can have a huge number of bookings for business functions during the week, visiting areas around business centers and certain times allows everyone to know you're coming so they will be ready and expect you. This kind of business works well when you visit construction sites, where they may be limited to sources of coffee, drinks and food due to their location. You will be a welcome site!

You can build a fantastic clientele just by being close to a school in the morning, when all those tired mothers dropping off their children will hail you as some kind of God for your presence, and coffee of course!

What kind of van you have is only limited to your imagination, there are many different designs, layouts, and ideas out there. Google is a great source of ideas for coffee and food vans.

The other beauty of having a van is you reduce your overheads substantially. If you find you are not in a financial position to have a store, a coffee van may be the answer to fulfilling your dream. As your mobile business grows, you may find you are in a better position to take on a retail premises as well as have your van. Suddenly your idea doubles, and you have both, and you come with a ready build in clientele and following as well.

Back to physical location advice:

First and foremost when choosing a location, you need to look at layout and access. There will always be something you can't change, yet there will always be something that you can improve to benefit your needs. In a coffee shop, access is critical. A dirty or unclean premises will obviously be able to be fixed and changed, lighting, and internal aspect, you can change. External aspects you can't so you must take all of this into consideration when deciding on what you want.

So now that you have your concept ideas of what kind of store you want, and you have sourced a few locations. It's time to analyze each one and look at the advantages and the disadvantages as they are presented. Below is a table that you can use as a guide to help you in this process. Don't limit yourself in your responses to single words, really put some time into finding somewhere that best suits your needs and your vision.

| Location -1 | Advantage | Disadvantage |
|---|---|---|
|  |  |  |
|  |  |  |
|  |  |  |
|  |  |  |
|  |  |  |

| Location -2 | Advantage | Disadvantage |
|---|---|---|
|  |  |  |
|  |  |  |
|  |  |  |
|  |  |  |

If you want to go into a deeper analysis, a SWOT Analysis is a great step forward. SWOT Analysis is also something your financers like to see, so working through this process really does help you solve some problems you may not have originally thought of. Take a look at the example below:

| Strengths (internal, positive factors) Strengths describe the positive attributes, tangible and intangible, of your organization. These are within your control. | Weaknesses (internal, negative factors) Weaknesses are aspects of your business that detract from the value you offer or place you at a competitive disadvantage |
|---|---|
| | |
| Opportunities (external, positive factors) Opportunities are external attractive factors that represent reasons for your business to exist and prosper | Threats (external, negative factors) Threats are external factors beyond your control that could put your business at risk. You may benefit from having contingency plans for them. |

Once you know the ideal location, time to start negotiating your lease. A commercial lease is very different than most residential leases. Most commercial leases are often quoted as per square feet in dollar amount which typically doesn't include CAM (Common Area Maintenance). You have to add both costs then multiply that number with your exact leased square footage to know what you will be paying.

Did you know that a commercial lease can have a clause where the landlord can get you out of business in just 30 days? How about the other clause where they can walk-in to your premises even when you are closed, and no one is at your location? Well, this is true, they can so it is always a good idea to have your lease reviewed by an attorney, so you know what is in that lease.

It is also a good idea to negotiate an exit strategy at least for the first year, so in the event, if your business doesn't flourish as you imagine, you can get out within the first year without having to pay any more penalties or other fees.

**COMMERCIAL LEASE AGREEMENT**

Date (For reference only): _____

_____

1. **PROPERTY:** Landlord rents to Tenant and Tenant rents from Landlord, the real property and improvements
   _____ comprise approximately _____ % of the total square footage of rentable space in the entire property. description of the Premises.
2. **TERM:** The term begins on (date) _____
   (Check A or B):
   - ☐ **A. Lease:** and shall terminate on (date) _____ at _____ term of this agreement expires, with Landlord's consent, shall create a month-to-month tenancy that paragraph 2B. Rent shall be at a rate equal to the rent for the immediately preceding month, conditions of this agreement shall remain in full force and effect.
   - ☐ **B. Month-to-month:** and continues as a month-to-month tenancy. Either party may terminate the tenancy least 30 days prior to the intended termination date, subject to any applicable laws. Such notice may be
   - ☐ **C. RENEWAL OR EXTENSION TERMS:** See attached addendum _____
3. **BASE RENT:**
   A. Tenant agrees to pay Base Rent at the rate of (CHECK ONE ONLY:)
   - ☐ (1) $ _____ per month, for the term of the agreement.
   - ☐ (2) $ _____ per month, for the first 12 months of the agreement. Commencing with each 12 months thereafter, rent shall be adjusted according to any increase in the U.S. Consumer

## DEMOGRAPHIC

It doesn't matter how wonderful your idea is for your new coffee shop if it is too far out of the way. Considering your foot traffic, drive through traffic opportunity, or parking near your site, is crucial to your business. Sometimes having a venue that is behind a large car park, yet within walking distance to remain convenient is a great space, somewhere that is in close proximity to a weekend market, or next to a court house, or office zone.

It all depends on what you want your space to be. Do you want simply sales? Or do you want to create the vibe where people want to go? Signage and street view is important too. Is your store on a busy road where you can see your store signs, so it has street presence? Do a lot of people have to walk past your store in order to get to a popular mall or a large car park?

Have you gone there a few times and watched the foot traffic? Spending time near your location choice is extremely important. You may, after a day or two, decide you don't like the area at all. Visit the stores that are around your location site and see how they feel to you. Are they quiet? Are they successful? Is there more activity at the other end of the street or mall that leaves your location flat and less frequented? These are all things to consider, and the only way you will really know this, is if you spend time at the location you are exploring. Your goal is to make choices that will impact your profitability in a positive way.

As I mentioned earlier, doing a thorough analysis of each proposed location is very vital. It is not only essential, but it is also beneficial to think about more out of the box competitors. These would be anyplace that would allow your targeted customers to get what you provide.

Look at places such as smoothie and juice bars, bakeries, or even fast food restaurants. These businesses are in different markets; they are all basically competing with the products you have.

Think about the businesses around your coffee shop; sometimes some of these companies can help you by actually complementing your offerings. Having your coffee shop near other businesses or a university could encourage students and employees to come to you first because of the added convenience of your location.

If you are near a mall or shopping center, you could receive traffic from those looking for a midday caffeine bump, while walking around and shopping.

## ACCESSIBILITY

Being a new and shiny business, you are bound to get first time customers. The aim of the game is to get repeat customers and great referrals. If you offer great product, they will come. If your place is hard to get to, is lacking parking, or is in an area of town that is less attractive, they may not come back.

Make sure that the visual of your store and the surrounding area is friendly, and well lit, also make sure that there is suitable parking available near your store. Look at what your competition is doing in the way of signage to help direct your customers to you.

Parking and access is the key to surviving in the industry, if you spend some time looking into locations that have these aspects, you are well on your way too success.

## BUILDING INFRASTRUCTURE

Unlike a retail store, coffee shops, cafes and restaurants need a specific kind of building infrastructure. It is important to make sure that your location has the ability to outfit a kitchen. The size and requirement of that kitchen will depend on your overall vision for your space.

If you are planning on just a take away venue, your requirements will be a lot less than one that has sit down tables, and different food choices to go with the coffee.

How many tables do you want? Have you thought about your capacity for seats? Does the venue have public toilets that will fit the licensing agreements for your kind of business? Does the framework of the premises have enough plumbing, electricity outlets and space to create your coffee shop?

Before wasting your time looking at a particular space, it is a good idea to have approached the management and asked about the basic terms. Making sure that your space is able to accommodate a food permit, or an alcohol license. Checking area restrictions and understanding the larger picture of what is required for setting up your business is where doing your own research comes into play.

Check with the local city or country business licensing office and find out what restrictions they have, and if your area of choice covers your needs.

There are so many things to consider when setting up a business. An important one, when looking at leases is affordability. If the space is everything you have ever wanted, yet the lease is higher than you have budgeted for, how are you going to justify your purchase? Your costs will always be transferred to your customer, and they may love your product, although it is cheaper elsewhere, so their decision not to turn your place into their local coffee shop, could be your prices.

Be aware of competitors in the area and what they charge for their coffee, what is it that will set you apart if you charge more due to higher lease costs? If you can't think of anything, or there isn't anything, you may need to reconsider the space.

You also need to think about whether a location needs any renovations. Small business loans are used to help cover building costs if you feel that renovations will leave you financially strained. Because it is a very big decision.

Most business owners will worry about taking out a business loan. When considering loan offers, there are quite a few things to check out. These things can include the total payback amount, ease of payback, and the lender's reputation. More on that little later.

After the cost of your building, there are a few lease terms you to be aware of that would help you figure out the best location for your shop. Here are some examples of these:

## LENGTH OF THE LEASE

Remember that commercial leases are real, legally binding contracts. You are generally unable to easily break or change any of the terms. Talk to a lawyer and get a full understanding before signing any agreements.

Read your lease and make sure you know if the landlord will be allowed to increase your rent after the lease is signed. Also, know the Insurance requirements. Different leases can require you to have a specific kind of insurance coverages that could increase your overall budget.

## SECURITY DEPOSIT

Make sure that you know conditions for your security deposit return. It is essential to understand how much you will have to pay upfront and the exact process of getting that security deposit back. It is important to know who is responsible for maintaining the space and who is responsible for the costs.

## NEGOTIATING THE COFFEE SHOP LEASE

You have to know what you want: In lease negation, your goal is to create a situation where everyone leaves feeling as they have won. It is your responsibility to know what you want and consistently pursue it.

Your potential landlord is looking out for their best interest, and you should know as well. If something is important to you, make sure to have it in writing. A verbal agreement won't be enough.

Your lease can be very limiting if you allow it to be. Make sure that what want is actually located somewhere in the language of your lease. Rank what you want in in three

1. Must Haves
2. Negotiable
3. Reaches

Remember that if you don't ask for it, you absolutely won't get it, the landlord is not a mind reader, you need to speak up now, this is absolutely critical.

Understand what your potential landlord wants: Listen to what their goals entail, and then modify your negotiations to meet their needs as well. Make sure to listen to what they are giving in too, and what they are fighting for. Remember that absolutely everything is negotiable, although show some discretion and restraint when considering what you want to negotiate, and it's not always money.

Sometimes the rent just can't be changed, but CAM, construction cost and other building costs might be able to be negotiated, do some research and find out how long the premises has been vacant, this could also be a great negotiating point to have partial construction costs covered.

Make sure that you have everything you want clearly written up for your landlord to consider, when talking to them over the phone, always follow up your conversation with an email recapping what you discussed so it is always in writing.

Length of the lease is also a factor that landlords take into consideration when working with you for remodeling and construction. As long as you have an exit clause and know what that will cost you if you break your lease early, this negotiation may help you keep your costs down.

Something else to consider when you have decided on your space is to find out from city if there are planned roadworks in the area. There is nothing worse than having your access blocked off. If there is construction and roadwork that could potentially impact your business down the track, ask your landlord if there will be a compromise for rent costs during this time.

# UNCLE SAM

## Name Your Business

What's in a name? The common question. In this case, a lot! Naming and Branding your new business is an important step for you to stand out among many. Making sure you have this concept in place when you are ready to launch is what will make you stand out immediately and identify you as individual amongst your competitors. So now, you need to think... what do I call my new business.

Some of the key things to take into consideration is relevance. You have two choices, you need to completely connect you name with your business concept, or your signage and branding. Your name should be easy to remember and be catchy in some way. Be unique, there are many ways to find your "Heavenly Grind."

Come up with five or six good names, and a branding idea. Now it is time to jump on Google. Put in your chosen name and see what shows up for you. If there is another business, move on, or change the wording around. Next you want to jump in and do a domain name search. Your online presence is an important one and owning your domain with the right name is important too.

If you have chosen to name your business "Heavenly Grind" you want to buy the domain name that goes with it, "heavenlygrind.com". You can also have TDL's and have your business domain registered as a ".net" or a ".biz". Buying all of these can prevent others from using your name with another TDL later. GoDaddy offers packages for buying complete domain names including other TDLs.

## INCORPORATING YOUR BUSINESS

Every business needs to have the proper license, permits and other authorizations to be able to perform its normal course of business. When you choose a legal entity for your coffee shop there are two main factors to consider:

- What you want
- The type of business model you intend to build

Often you have the option of choosing to file as a limited liability company or LLC, general partnership or even sole proprietorship. A sole proprietorship is the ideal business structure for someone starting a coffee shop, especially if it is a moderate start from your home. However, most prefer the benefits of an LLC.

If you plan to eventually expand your coffee shop to other locations or potentially online, then you definitely don't want to file as a sole proprietor. In this instance, you should definitely file as an LLC.

When you file as an LLC, you will be able to protect yourself from personal liability. This means that if anything goes wrong while operating your business then only the money you invested into the company is at risk.

This isn't the case if you file as a sole proprietor or a general partnership. LLCs are simple and flexible to operate since you won't need a board of directors, shareholder meetings or other managerial formalities in order to run your business.

Here are all the legal business structures you can choose from, it is best to get some advice from your CPA or accountant or an attorney.

## LEGAL BUSINESS STRUCTURE

When starting a business, there are five different business structures you can choose from:

- Sole Proprietor

- Partnership

- Corporation (Inc. or Ltd.)

- S Corporation

- Limited Liability Company (LLC)

## SOLE PROPRIETOR

This is not the safest structure for a coffee shop. It is used for a business owned by a single person or a married couple. Under this structure, the owner is personally liable for all business debts and may file their personal income tax.

## PARTNERSHIP

If your business is owned and operated by multiple people, when it comes to structuring your business, you can choose one of two kinds of partnerships. These two kinds of partnerships are general partnerships and limited partnerships.

In a general partnership, the partners manage the business together and are responsible for each other debts. A limited partnership actually has both limited and general partners.

The general partners work as previously described, but the limited partners are only investors that don't actually have any control over the company and are not responsible for the debts in the same way.

## CORPORATION (INC. OR LTD.)

The corporate structure is complex and costs quite a bit more money than most other business structures. This is because a corporation is a completely independent legal entity. It is separate from its owners. It also requires you to comply with more regulations and requirements.

A corporation provides increased liability protection for the business owner or owners. A corporation's debt is not considered that of its owners. This lessens your personal risk.

It isn't a very common structure among coffee shop since there are shares of stocks involved.

Profits are taxes both are at the corporate level and distributed to shareholders. When you structure a business at this level, there are often lawyers involved.

## S CORPORATION

This is one of the most popular types of business entity people forms to it avoid double taxation. It is taxed similarly to a partnership entity. But an S Corp. needs to be approved to be classified as such, so it isn't very common among coffee shops.

The S corporation is going to be a more attractive option for small-business owners than a regular corporation. That's because an S corporation takes some great parts of what a corporation offers on a smaller, less expensive scale. It has some very appealing tax benefits as well as provides business owners with the liability protection of a corporation.

You have a couple of choices when it comes to filing the necessary paperwork for your business. The first is to have a lawyer or accountant to file a legal business entity for you.

You can also do it yourself using online resources, or by going to your local city office and filling out the necessary paperwork. You can go on websites like leaglzoom.com and draw up the document for less money than what an attorney would charge you to do the same.

## LIMITED LIABILITY COMPANY (LLC)

This is the most common business structure among coffee shops. It offers benefits for small businesses since it reduces the risk of losing all your personal assets in case you are faced with a lawsuit. It provides a clear separation between business and personal assets. You can also elect to be taxed as a corporation, which saves you money come tax time.

If you are unsure which specific business structure you should choose then, you can discuss it with an accountant. They will direct you to the best possible option for what your business goals are. You will find a sample articles of incorporation at the end of the book. Just remember you should always get some sound legal advice when filing your corporation.

I filed my first LLC via Legalzoom.com as I didn't have the extra funds to hire an attorney. Thankfully it worked out well for me.

## APPLY AND OBTAIN YOUR EMPLOYER IDENTIFICATION NUMBER FROM IRS

EIN or Employer Identification number is essentially a social security or tax identification number but for your business. IRS and many other governmental agencies can identify your business via this unique nine-digit number.

Remember you will not need this number if you choose to be a sole proprietorship for your business.

It is simple to apply, either you can do it yourself or get your accountant to apply for you, but the process is simple, you fill out the form SS-4, which can be filed online, via Fax or via mail.

Here is a link to IRS website where you can download or fill out the form online.

https://www.irs.gov/businesses/small-businesses-self-employed/how-to-apply-for-an-ein

# Form SS-4

## Application for Employer Identification Number

**Form SS-4**
(Rev. January 2010)
Department of the Treasury
Internal Revenue Service

(For use by employers, corporations, partnerships, trusts, estates, churches, government agencies, Indian tribal entities, certain individuals, and others.)

► See separate instructions for each line. ► Keep a copy for your records.

OMB No. 1545-0003

EIN

| | |
|---|---|
| 1 | Legal name of entity (or individual) for whom the EIN is being requested |

Type or print clearly.

| | | | |
|---|---|---|---|
| 2 | Trade name of business (if different from name on line 1) | 3 | Executor, administrator, trustee, "care of" name |
| 4a | Mailing address (room, apt., suite no. and street, or P.O. box) | 5a | Street address (if different) (Do not enter a P.O. box.) |
| 4b | City, state, and ZIP code (if foreign, see instructions) | 5b | City, state, and ZIP code (if foreign, see instructions) |
| 6 | County and state where principal business is located | | |
| 7a | Name of responsible party | 7b | SSN, ITIN, or EIN |

| | |
|---|---|
| 8a | Is this application for a limited liability company (LLC) (or a foreign equivalent)? ☐ Yes ☐ No |
| 8b | If 8a is "Yes," enter the number of LLC members ► |
| 8c | If 8a is "Yes," was the LLC organized in the United States? ☐ Yes ☐ No |

**9a** Type of entity (check only one box). Caution. If 8a is "Yes," see the instructions for the correct box to check.

☐ Sole proprietor (SSN) _____
☐ Partnership
☐ Corporation (enter form number to be filed) ►
☐ Personal service corporation
☐ Church or church-controlled organization
☐ Other nonprofit organization (specify) ►
☐ Other (specify) ►

☐ Estate (SSN of decedent)
☐ Plan administrator (TIN)
☐ Trust (TIN of grantor)
☐ National Guard ☐ State/local government
☐ Farmers' cooperative ☐ Federal government/military
☐ REMIC ☐ Indian tribal governments/enterprises
Group Exemption Number (GEN) if any ►

| | | | |
|---|---|---|---|
| 9b | If a corporation, name the state or foreign country (if applicable) where incorporated | State | Foreign country |

**10** Reason for applying (check only one box)
☐ Started new business (specify type) ►
☐ Hired employees (Check the box and see line 13.)
☐ Compliance with IRS withholding regulations
☐ Other (specify) ►

☐ Banking purpose (specify purpose) ►
☐ Changed type of organization (specify new type) ►
☐ Purchased going business
☐ Created a trust (specify type) ►
☐ Created a pension plan (specify type) ►

| | |
|---|---|
| 11 | Date business started or acquired (month, day, year). See instructions. |
| 12 | Closing month of accounting year |
| 13 | Highest number of employees expected in the next 12 months (enter -0- if none). If no employees expected, skip line 14. |
| 14 | If you expect your employment tax liability to be $1,000 or less in a full calendar year and want to file Form 944 annually instead of Forms 941 quarterly, check here. (Your employment tax liability generally will be $1,000 or less if you expect to pay $4,000 or less in total wages.) If you do not check this box, you must file Form 941 for every quarter. ☐ |

| Agricultural | Household | Other |
|---|---|---|
| | | |

**15** First date wages or annuities were paid (month, day, year). Note. If applicant is a withholding agent, enter date income will first be paid to nonresident alien (month, day, year). ►

**16** Check one box that best describes the principal activity of your business.
☐ Construction ☐ Rental & leasing ☐ Transportation & warehousing
☐ Real estate ☐ Manufacturing ☐ Finance & insurance
☐ Health care & social assistance ☐ Wholesale-agent/broker
☐ Accommodation & food service ☐ Wholesale-other ☐ Retail
☐ Other (specify) ►

**17** Indicate principal line of merchandise sold, specific construction work done, products produced, or services provided.

**18** Has the applicant entity shown on line 1 ever applied for and received an EIN? ☐ Yes ☐ No
If "Yes," write previous EIN here ►

| | | |
|---|---|---|
| **Third Party Designee** | Complete this section only if you want to authorize the named individual to receive the entity's EIN and answer questions about the completion of this form. | |
| | Designee's name | Designee's telephone number (include area code) |
| | Address and ZIP code | Designee's fax number (include area code) |

Under penalties of perjury, I declare that I have examined this application, and to the best of my knowledge and belief, it is true, correct, and complete.

Name and title (type or print clearly) ►

Applicant's telephone number (include area code)

Applicant's fax number (include area code)

This is one important step, but it can only be done after you have a fully executed article of incorporation which has been approved by the state, and you have an EIN number assigned by the IRS.

Once you have these two documents, you should be able to go to a bank and open your first commercial bank account.

But remember to check and understand various types of commercial checking account fees, you want to find a bank that offers free or almost free commercial checking account because some larger banks can charge you hundreds of dollars each month depending on how many transactions you do. Make sure to ask and shop around before you sign on the dotted line.

Since you are opening a food-related retail business, one of the most essential steps in your licensing process should be to discuss your proposed plan and operation with your local county health department. As they will be the ultimate authority to issue you a food permit without which you can operate your business.

Next step would be to go to your local city and county business licensing office and find out what type of business and regulatory licenses you are required to have. It should take a few days to get your licenses and permits in place, and then you are finally and officially in business.

You also need to attend a 4-6-hour class to obtain your SafeServ permit. This is a certificate that ensures that the manager or the owner of any food-related businesses know how to handle food safely.

Each establishment needs to have minimum one person who is certified in the SafeServ program.

Time to decide what you want to sell out of your coffee shop. If you are a coffee drinker, you I am sure already have an idea of what you want to see in your coffee shop. But remember to make your business truly profitable, there are other related items you need to sell that are not COFFEE.

For example, some food and drink items for kids that will accompany their parents. How about for grownups that do not drink coffee?

How about tea drinkers? How about snacks, cookies, cakes and a few finger food items? Take a look at a Starbucks; they now sell sandwiches, breakfast and so many other foods and non-food related items.

Some of your research can be done right on the internet. Once you decide what should be on your menu board, time to design and order your menu board. For this, you can contact any of your local sign shops, show them a design or two and see if they can create something similar.

On the other hand, if you want your menu to be unique, you have to hire a graphic designer and have it all draw up in Auto-Cad from which your sign company can build it.

Here is a place where I had one of my menu designed. 99designs.com.

The best thing about this place, you can have many designers bid on your project and show you a mockup design, you pick the best looking one and pay only one designer not 20 of them. The cost is less than $500.

# DÉCOR, FURNITURE & EQUIPMENT

There are so many things to consider when opening a coffee shop, but don't forget what the place actually looks like. The aesthetics of a coffee shop is also important. The decor and presentation are what often attracts new customers to give your place a try.

Ideally, you want a design that appeals to a wide variety of people to attract a variety of customers to your coffee shop for maximum sales, so keep this in mind during your decorating plans.

Think about creating various sections in the coffee shop, so the whole room isn't just a bunch of tables, chairs, and loveseats. You want to make sure that the shop has a section that has tables, and another with loveseats and plusher chairs. This will give your customers different seating choices.

Having a table or a display of additional coffee related items, they can purchase for home would work well in any space as well.

These products could be specialized coffee beans, espresso machines, coffee syrups or another type of merchandise.

Some examples of great merchandise are t-shirts and sweatshirts with the coffee shop's logo and slogan as well as coffee mugs and to-go thermoses. Have this table very close to the checkout counter. This will encourage impulse purchase and give those standing in line some interesting things to look at.

The goal for your Coffee shops is to aim to provide a relaxing environment. This goal should be aft your décor choices. The walls must reflect the calming mood or tone the coffee shop is trying to evoke. One way that this can be achieved is to use local artists' paintings or photography on the walls. This can help in a variety of ways. Connecting to other local business such as galleries is a great way to get started drumming up business, and artwork can be beautiful and relaxing to look at.

Another very cool option is to add things that would normally not be considered art and hang these items on the walls as art pieces, such as an old car or motorcycle parts, tools, and supplies used on coffee plantations, or vintage record covers. Having exciting things on your walls encourages people to stay and look around.

Finally, a very on theme idea is to display beautiful photography which could include coffee beans or images of the cultivation and roasting process.

I hired a local interior decorator who charged me $2,400, but she did an excellent job is coming up with ideas for wall color, flooring ideas, wall décor and furniture suggestions all of which were within my tight budget. So, you may consider going that route as well.

## CREATIVE LIGHTING

Something that is overlooked in the choosing of decor is lighting choices. The lighting in the coffee shop is also part of the decoration process. To begin, think about how much lightening you want, you could have each table have its own hanging lamp that is extended from the ceiling, which can be dimmed at night for a cozier setting.

Each table may also have smaller candles to provide a relaxing atmosphere. Remember a creative lighting plan can shine your coffee shop and make it more inviting, cozy and comfortable for your customers.

## TABLE DECORATIONS

Because The tables in a coffee shop are frequently used, therefore, you need to keep them clutter free and clean. So any and all tabletop decorations would most likely be out of the question.

However, a very cool idea to go around this issue would be to choose tables that allow you to add decorations underneath the glass surface, so your customers see the decorations when they sit down. For example, you could create a collage of coffee related images, or take fresh coffee beans and spread them around before placing the glass top.

## THEMES CAN BE A LOT OF FUN

If you choose a theme for your coffee shop, it can help target your decor choices and make your shop more brandable. A theme can open you up to many options. You can create a mural on the wall of coffee plants growing at sunset.

Your tables can have bits of historical information under them, or, coffee beans with labels indicating the different places they are from. You can integrate any theme, with a little creative flair. If it's a musical theme, then consider putting in an old-style jukebox that people can play music from.

This is a basic outline of how anyone can come up with a design for a coffee shop that works well for space and location. Having an inviting and fun atmosphere is one element that can really keep your business thriving.

## COMPETITION RESEARCH

Before deciding on what trendy décor and furniture and fixtures you want to have you in your coffee shop, it is a good idea to take a tour of a few coffee shops in your extended area of say 150 miles. This way you can get a great idea what you like and what you don't. Take detail note of what you want in your shop. If possible take a few pictures so you can later show them to your interior designer.

This is also time to start looking for gently used furniture from reputable used restaurant equipment supply companies. You can find most of their inventory online, so it is easy for you to see if the color and design matches what you are looking for.

Buying them used can save you over 50% compared to buying them new. Same goes for equipment as well.

When opening a coffee shop, there are so many things you need to make it work. Having the right equipment to both make the coffee and to run the coffee shop are essential. This chapter will discuss the main items that you will need to have to make your coffee shop a success.

Before buying anything, you'll first want to figure out if you are planning to buy the equipment upfront or if you prefer a lease option. The choice to lease or buy will have a significant impact on the budget.

Leasing equipment allows you to free up cash flow, but reading the fine print is essential. You don't want to end up paying significantly more in the long run. I personally do not prefer the leasing option but wanted to mention it, so you will know that there is that option out there.

Once you've decided on whether to buy or lease, or maybe a bit of both, you can now start to choose your vendors. Begin the search for vendor the simplest way with a simple Google search for coffee shop equipment vendors. This will enable you to look at both local and national vendors that will get you started on the right foot.

Another great option is going out of business sales. Opening a business can be difficult so unfortunately, this is a viable way to obtain the equipment you need.

When a business closes, they often try to sell their equipment to get back as much money as they possibly can before they have to close their doors. So if you know of any restaurants or other food service providers near you that are closing, try tracking down the owner and see if they would be interested in selling any of the equipment they currently have. If they are, you can often purchase the equipment they have at significantly discounted prices.

Using Social media and digital yard sales is another way to go. This has really become a very popular option in today's age. Social media platforms like Facebook and Twitter now offer online marketplaces where you can sell any items both household and commercial items you no longer want. There are also online platforms totally dedicated to this type of selling the popular app, let go.

Finally, there are equipment auctions. This is a great a great source for buying coffee shop equipment. There are companies hold auctions all across the country for all kinds' restaurant equipment.

They would be a heavily discounted process. You could luck out and be able to practice several pieces of much needed this way. This is an amazing option if you can find one within driving distance. Even if you have to driveways, it is worth taking a ride over there and seeing what kind of discounts are available.

## 12 MUST- HAVE EQUIPMENT TYPES OF YOUR COFFEE SHOP

### 1. AUTOMATIC DRIP COFFEE MAKERS

This is the first thing on the list because it is basic, but often times overlooked. You can expect that about a third of your customers will order drip coffee over any other drink that is available.

You want a high-quality, durable coffee maker, that will be able to withstand all of that use. It also needs to quick enough to meet demand at the busiest times for customers which will more than likely be morning for coffee.

(Credit – Bunn.com)

It also has to be big enough to produce large batches of coffee so that you aren't always brewing coffee throughout the day. You will want to have more than one automatic drip coffee makers.

This is because different customers will desire different roasts. It is suggested that you have three to four coffee makers with different blends. This will keep you from having to constantly make new batches of coffee, without spreading yourself too thin in busy times.

I want to recommend the brand call Bunn here that has been time tested for many years and for thousands of coffee shops around the world. Even if you to pay a few hundred extra bucks for this brand, go for it, they are truly the best coffee makers out there for commercial use.

## 2. HIGH-QUALITY ESPRESSO MACHINE

The typical coffee drinks that your customers are likely to order usually have an element of espresso, either by itself or in combination with steamed milk. This means that you have to have a high-quality espresso machine. This is a piece of equipment that will not come cheap, unfortunately. The industrial espresso machine market is full of very expensive pieces of equipment that are bound to bust a budget or two.

So it's important to understand what makes any espresso machine a great espresso machine and how to shop smart and with your budget in mind to get the best value when you find what you feel is the right one for you.

# 3. COMMERCIAL COFFEE GRINDER

Most coffee shops keep beans in inventory to account for the freshness of their coffee. These beans are usually stored in a cool, dry place like a basement. Because you want to serve very fresh coffee, you want to grind those beans right before making each new pot of coffee.

That means adding an industrial coffee grinder to your equipment list is very important. Most people do not understand that the right coffee grinder can make such a large difference in the different flavor profiles and aromas of your coffee and espresso. That is why it's very important to invest in the right coffee grinder.

# 4. MILK AND WATER

These two items can make or break your coffee. Having the very best of these items can make your coffee better. The milk to need to be fresh and the highest quality possible.

The water needs to be the purest you can buy. Having either your water or milk be subpar can very much lead to a subpar product.

When considering the water you use to make all your coffee and drinks, consider a simple water filtration system.

This will reduce the mineral content and protect your espresso machine because of the higher the mineral content, the harder the machine works. This also increases the chance of damaging various coffee making equipment.

When you open your coffee shop, you'll have food to keep fresh and dairy products to refrigerate. This requires refrigeration both in display cases and counter fridge units behind the counter. Refrigeration must be taken into consideration when you design your coffee shop.

It must be aesthetically pleasing but streamlined enough for the baristas to quickly make customers' drinks. You'll also want the display cases and other refrigeration units to stay within the theme of the room and not jeopardize the streamlined bar areas. Regardless of what type of coffee or food you decide to serve in your coffee shop, a refrigeration system is a must-have to include on your coffee shop equipment list.

## 5. CONTAINERS, PUMPS AND ASSORTED MISCELLANEOUS

Since coffee shops the use of a lot of beans and a huge selection of drink toppings, you must have the hardware to effectively use and store these items. This means pumps for all the syrups, boxes and crates to conveniently store coffee beans near your coffee makers and simple answers to all the storage issues that plague some coffee shops.

If you don't have an effective system for storage, your business will run less efficiently, driving you and your employee's crazy, as well as diminishing profits over the long run. Partner with a local or reliable restaurant supply retailer, buy in bulk and plan your system out carefully and effectively.

(Credit – Zesco.com)

If your coffee shop has a small selection of hot food, which one survey found is the case with at least 60 percent of coffee and tea shops out there, you'll need a reliable way to prepare your food quickly, so as not to hold up the efficiency of your operation.

Most stores serve breakfast sandwiches, or at least bagels and pastries, which will necessitate either a conveyor toaster or a pop-up model. If you have frozen breakfast sandwiches, similar to big chains like Starbucks, you'll want a quick but compact oven (or two) that baristas have easy access to without clogging the entire front-of-house operation.

## 8. SECURITY SYSTEM

Every mercantile business needs an excellent system to deter crime in and around their business. This may include security equipment such as cameras, burglar.

In addition, consider implementing systems for proper oversight to prevent employees from helping themselves to too much of your product, giving away too many complimentary drinks, or lifting cash from the register.

There are a wide variety of choices on the market for security products and surveillance equipment. You'll want to find a company that will oversee installation and has experience and expertise preventing crime near your business.

Profit loss from theft or other calamity is something you don't need as you enter the market with a new store.

## 9. SHELVING

One of the most underrepresented and under-appreciated items on a coffee shop equipment list is adequate shelving.

Most coffee shops sell merchandise, bulk coffee, mugs, and coffee equipment like French presses and other accessories as a way to make additional money outside of the primary business of slinging drinks.

Both in the public area of the store and behind the counter for the convenience of the baristas, shelving is a must. Convenient shelf units can be the difference between a coffee shop that doesn't have the space to allow much seating and appears cluttered and chaotic and one that is aesthetically pleasing.

Additionally, if the baristas in your shop don't have proper storage, essential items will have to be stored farther away, hurting their ability to remain quick and efficient with customers.

In my opinion, one of the best and cheapest place to pick up great quality stainless steel commercial shelving is Sam's club. I buy all my shelving from there. You may want to check and compare their prices with other retailers.

## 10.    FREEZERS AND COLD PRODUCT STORAGE

If you do intend to follow the ever-successful Starbucks model for food and drink combinations, you'll need freezers, both in the front of your coffee shop where your baristas work, as well as in the back where inventory is stored.

A selection of frozen food that can be flash-baked in the oven should be kept up front for baristas to have easy access to orders. Since frozen food is easy to store and has a long shelf life, you should store a surplus in the back, so you never run out. You don't want to have to tell customers that you can't serve them something on the menu.

## 11.    A FEW INDUSTRIAL BLENDERS

Today, it's no secret that blended drinks, especially seasonal drinks, are all the rage among coffee consumers. You'll need at least one blender to capitalize on the blended frozen drink craze. These blenders have to hold up well to a lot of use every day because frozen drinks are so popular. They also have to be industrial in nature in order to break down the ice as will any add-ins.

## 12. POS SYSTEM AND RELATED HARDWARE

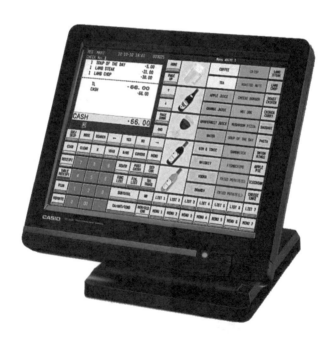

Without an efficient and reliable point of sale system, your business can be slowed down by lags in payment processing, poor inventory management and untimely services and repairs. But if your POS is cloud-based, you won't have to worry about tracking your data or inventory because the system will help you do it all. Luckily, cloud-based POS systems are not only lightning fast, but reliable as well.

But these systems are so much more than bundles of software and hardware. In one ergonomic terminal, you will also have the power to track your business' analytics and profits, keep track of inventory, and oversee email marketing to bring in new customers.

You may not need all items on this coffee shop equipment list, or just a few. There is no absolute recipe for success when opening a coffee shop. To understand what will work for you, be aware of the demographic you are serving as well as their needs and wants. Do not buy equipment that you do not need or are unsure about how to use them.

When buying new equipment always be aware of the wide- eye syndrome. Let's face it some things just look cool, and we want them, but this is not the place for impulse buying. That money would be better spent on things you really need. Buying things that appear fancy and high-tech will lead you nowhere.

Here are some links to a few websites where you can get great POS systems for a decent price for your coffee shop. Don't worry, most of these POS systems can be customized to exactly what you want in a POS.

https://www.shopkeep.com/business-types/coffee-shop-pos

https://squareup.com/pos/coffee-shop

Here is a blog post from a very helpful site from Coffee shop business owners about POS systems for Coffee shop Startups. Read through it and you will learn a lot.

https://coffeeshopstartups.com/best-coffee-shop-pos-system/

## FINDING NEW & USED EQUIPMENT FOR YOUR COFFEE SHOP

Here are some places you can look for great used coffee making equipment online. Please understand that I am not an affiliate for any of these companies, so do your research and compare prices before buying.

http://www.ebay.com/bhp/used-restaurant-equipment

https://www.acitydiscount.com/

http://kescoflorida.com/

https://www.webstaurantstore.com/restaurant-equipment.html

http://www.jeansrestaurantsupply.com/restaurant-equipment/used-restaurant-equipment.html

In addition, you can also search your local newspaper, craigslist and local in town used equipment dealers.

# PLANNING & BUILD-OUT

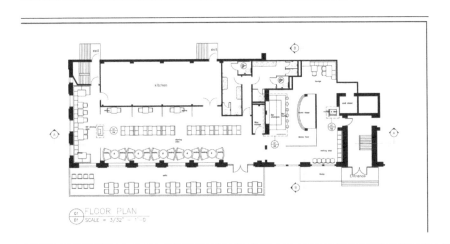

FLOOR PLAN
SCALE = 3/32" = 1'-0"

## PLANNING STAGE

As I mentioned earlier, depending on your city, county and state's requirements, and the location you are trying to lease, you may be required to submit some type of plans of what you are trying to accomplish.

It could be as little as a simple hand-drawn plan for your local county health department showing what and how you will lay out all your kitchen equipment. If you are planning on installing a certain type of cooking equipment such as a commercial fryer or a grill, then you may be required to install a commercial ventilation hood system. So be aware of that as it can get very expensive very fast.

Your best bet would be to first think about what food item you want to sell at your location along with coffee. My advice is not to get into a grill or fryer as they do require so much more changes to an existing building unless that building was a restaurant before and has a place for a grill or fryer along with a proper vent hood system in place.

Once you know what you will be selling, start with your local county health department and ask to see what their requirements are for issuing you a food permit.

In the event, if you need a total makeover, meaning you are asked to rebuild a whole interior of a building (total build-out), you will need to hire an architect to get a set of plans drawn. But for this to happen, you will need to furnish specific information to your architect.

1. How many seating you want in the facility
2. A list of all equipment you will be using along with their specs so an electrical design can be drawn based on the actual load.
3. How many restrooms you will need

4. What type of lighting fixtures you prefer to install
5. If you will need any walk-in cooler or freezer in the facility
6. All plumbing requirements according to the health department code (if you will need a three compartment sink, a mop sick, etc.)
7. A layout of your counters and checkout stand
8. Exact area of placement for all your reach-in coolers

Once you provide such information, the architect will then start drawing up the all the plans along with an HVAC plan based on the current city or county code.

Once they are done with the plan, they will send it off to your city or county building inspector for proper approval. Once the set of plans are approved, then your work will start.

Time for you to either hire a general contractor, or if it is allowed in your city, you can act as the general contractor and hire sub-contractors to finish various jobs that need to be done according to the plan.

For example, you can hire a licensed plumber to do all the plumbing work, hire an HVAC company to get all your AC related work done and so on.

Last time I had to get a full set of plans for a franchise fast food restaurant, it cost me around $10,000, but that was a full set of plans which included everything from wall décor to HVAC and all everything in between.

Before you get all nervous, let me assure you, if you are just opening a coffee shop, chances are you won't have to do all that. But I wanted to mention this because in certain city or state all these may be requirements based on what you are renting.

It may not be a bad idea to discuss your goal and plans with the city or county health board to get an idea of what might be involved this way you will be better prepared for what will come next.

## BUILD-OUT

This is a stage where you see your coffee shop coming to life little by little. Whatever you envisioned it to be, you will now see it coming together piece by piece.

Regardless if you hired a general contractor or an interior designer, but this is the stage where things will happen fast. So make sure to have all your ducks in a row.

Make sure to install/place all your big equipment before installing the counter tops, this way you won't have any gaps or holes. Get any and all HVAC, plumbing and electrical work done.

Test out all your electrical components to make sure everything is in working condition. Once that is done, time to start painting the walls. Hang all the decors once you are done the painting.

But before you bring in furniture, time to start laying your floor tiles or wood planks, whichever you picked. Let the floor settle for a few days before bringing the furniture.

Once you are done with all this, time to call on your health and building inspector for their final inspection so you can get the CO (certificate of occupancy) without which you cannot open your business.

# MANAGEMENT AND EMPLOYEES

Hiring staff is one of the most important aspects of your business. It is important to get this right at the beginning. You can have the best coffee in the world, although the customer will remember the way the staff treated them, the way they looked, the way they smiled (or didn't), how much they engaged them and that will become the memory imbedded. This is your key to success. You can be particular in the search for who you want to be your front end, and back end. Personalities clashing in a business environment is a proven vibe killer, and in a coffee shop, you want upbeat and happy staff, that is the key to upbeat and happy customers!  Below is a 10-step process on how to hire your staff. This principle is across the board for most businesses, although there are some key tips on employing staff that are in the business of serving customers food and beverage.

## 10 STEP PROCESS ON HOW TO HIRE, TRAIN AND RETAIN EMPLOYEES.

- Where and how to find the right people to hire?

- Asking the right question during interview

- Providing proper training

- Employee appearance

- Motivating and empowering your employees

- Teaching them marketing 101

- Rewarding the right behavior

- How to discipline bad behavior

- Setting up Target & goal-oriented incentives

- Regular employee meetings and coaching

Firstly, think about the vibe you have created in your coffee shop. How does it look, how does it feel? What kind of people are starting to come to your store, what would they expect in a server? Good Baristas need good training. They need to understand individual wants and tastes of the customers. There is nothing worse than paying 5 dollars for a coffee only to have the wrong order handed to you and hear your name screamed out mis-pronounced.

Having a coffee made by a fully trained barista is very different from receiving a generic drink. Coffee that is steeped at the wrong temperature burns, your staff must know this, or you must be prepared to train them the way you want your product presented.

At this stage, you become much more than the owner of the business, you have to manage recruiting, have management strategies and guidelines in place, you also have disciplinary processes in place in case you encounter issues with your staff.

Reducing your workload will help you to stay motivated in your business. Taking on too much work will burn you out. Learning to identify key staff at the beginning of your search is vital, as they will be able to help you find and manage staff as you move forward.

Knowing exactly what you need in staff is a key. You will need to have

- Front of house – who interact with your customers and handle money
- Cooks if you have cooked and food preparation
- Support staff, to keep things running behind the scenes
- Cleaning staff

You may be able to interweave some of these jobs together, and you may have rotation shifts, where someone from one of these rolls will prove competent to manage the other staff members in your absence.

It is hard to entrust others to be a part of your business. Sound accounting and stocktaking is a must, as this is a huge part of managing staff and encompassing staffing issues.

You may encounter some staff members that are unable to come in often due to other commitments such as school, or college. These people are great for a list of seasonal times, and you will be able to extend your staffing needs. Never discount a staff member who has limited availability, as they may be the perfect person to call in at a pinch, or for seasonal busy rushes.

If you have decided that your coffee shop could benefit from taking on staff, the next step you have to take is to advertise. Before doing this, it's important to consider the type of person that would be well suited to fulfill your shop's needs.

Baristas and waiting staff have to interact with clients. They need to be able to have a fast conversation, and multi task, keeping the mind on the job and also keeping their eye and ear on the customer. Look for staff who remember names to be front end. A returning customer greeted by name feels good every time.

Those who work in your kitchen will most likely have had some experience in that area. This can be a very high-pressure placement, so it may be possible to take on a trained staff member and have a support staff member who they can train for you, and then, eventually train others and so forth. Again, looking for your key staff in the areas you need help will be the foundation of your business staffing moving forward.

Advertising for staff is an important factor. As you receive their resumes, tick of what you feel are their strong points. Have they worked with the public? Do they have Barista and serving experience? Are they a people person? How is their spelling and grammar? Now you can vet the applicants and meet with them, asking questions, and importantly, waiting for them to ask you questions.

Make sure you have a "Scope of work" document for each position, so that your staff know what they are to do. If you have a particular way you want your dishes stacked, rinsed, and sanitized, make sure they know your requirements. These may be different to where they have worked in the past, yet, they now work for you, so they have to do things your way. If you give each position a scope of work, then you are covered if later you decide they are not a good fit due to not conforming to your wants and needs.

Working out the best times for staff to be on and rotation shift rosters will be your next project. Make sure that you have experienced staff in at the busiest times and where possible a support staff that can be trained. If you get this right early, and stay on top of rostering, you will do well.

With every business, there is no guarantee that staff will perform to the level you expect. Make sure you know what your state laws are regarding staff. Can you give them a trial period? How long is that? Write up a disciplinary procedure and have all the information about being hired well documented and given to your new staff at the point of hire. If they read your documents as is required and they are not aware of procedure, you as an employer have done the right thing, and it is on the staff member to agree to the terms of their employment.

You may need to deal with:

- Poor or slow performance
- Negative customer interaction
- Poor Hygiene
- Poor attendance
- Argumentative
- Disruptive behavior towards other staff

As the owner and manager, you have the responsibility to address any kinds of issues with your employees so in a way you become a guidance counselor, working through issues with staff just like you would a classroom. Then you need to discover the cause of the problem and a potential resolution with them. Sometimes, it may be a simple case of moving a staff member to a different shift, so they don't have to interact with another employee. There are times when you are going to have to let someone go.

When firing staff, make sure that you have given them written warnings, and also that you are up to date on the laws of your state regarding the steps recommended, and the proper procedure. If you have senior staff in your buisiness already, make sure they are aware of what has happened so they can calm, or stop any other disharmony from happening within other staff members. Consider any potential legal implcations that you may have when you fire someone.

Again, I can't reiterate enough, make sure that all interactions on the road to firing staff is documented and in writing!

Customer service and engagement are always a place for improvements. There's always something that you can do to make your coffee shop more welcoming to your customers. Regular staff meetings are a great way to get on top of staffing problems and also to find solutions for better ways things can be done. Never underestimate or overlook staff opinion when it comes to ideas, you may end up with the best one yet.

Understanding conflict resolution and developing policies for your staff is a great way to better understand what is needed when your customers are not happy too. If everyone working for you knows your policy for conflict resolution, their attitude towards the customer who isn't happy with the service will improve.

Staffing is all about communication.

For online employee training here are few sites that have shown great results.

http://www.itsimulations.com/training-courses/online-restaurant-training/

http://www.restauranttraininguniversity.com/

http://servicethatsells.com/online-restaurant-training/

https://www.restaurantowner.com/public/Restaurant-Training-Manual-Templates.cfm

# CHOOSING THE RIGHT FOOD AND COFFEE VENDOR

Making great tasting coffee starts with quality coffee beans. The beans are essential in cultivating the flavor and complexity of the final product. Finding the best beans isn't hard, as long as you know what you are looking for. This section of the book will show you what to look for in quality beans.

Choosing Your Bean type first thing to know about coffee beans is that there are two of them. What I mean by this is that there are two distinct species of coffee beans: Arabica and Robusta. These two bean varieties taste very different and therefore are used very differently. Arabica coffee beans are the sweeter coffee beans of the two.

They have a milder flavor because of the sweetness; The Robusta coffee beans can also have nuanced flavors such as notes of fruit, and chocolate. Robusta coffee beans are the kinds of coffee beans that are used in instant coffee, because of the milder flavor Arabica beans are not ideal for most types of instant coffee. Knowing the differences between the two beans will help you purchase coffee beans whose characteristics meet your taste expectations.

## ARABICA VS. ROBUSTA

Arabica coffee beans are grown and harvested at high altitudes. Their cultivation can be compared to the cultivation of grapes at a vineyard. You can very easily tell the difference between Arabica and Robusta coffee beans. They actually have twice the amount of chromosomes as Robusta coffee beans.

They are a deep green compared to the light green or brown color of Robusta beans, and they are quite a bit larger. Robusta beans are definitely easier to cultivate. Arabica beans produce a considerably better brew whose flavors will be milder, more aromatic, and not as bitter as those produced by Robusta beans.

This is what makes Arabica blends delicious, but also more expensive to obtain and use. Robusta beans are really all about function. They are nowhere near as delicate as Arabica beans, and much more affordable to grow in large qualities.

However, they lack all the wonderful qualities that Arabica beans possess. To compensate for this, the beans they produce are oftentimes used for blends. Sometimes the combination of Arabica and Robusta is just right for lighter roasts.

## LOCATION, LOCATION, LOCATION

You might not think about this when it comes to coffee beans but where a coffee bean is grown will determine their flavor characteristics upon brewing no matter how darkly they are roasted or how they are brewed. The soil and atmosphere are so different that it has a huge impact on what the bans end up tasting like.

Generally, there are three world regions where the finest coffee beans originate, from and each region produces coffee with unique and distinct flavors. Here are some popular places that coffee beans are grown, and why they are such effect on places for growing.

## LATIN AMERICA

The beans that come from places such as Columbia, South America, Costa Rica, and Mexico have distinct flavors that are perfect for mild to medium roasts.

Their flavors are sweet and light but balanced with the right amount of acidity that makes it a delicious brew. Coffee from beans grown in this part of the world works well with breakfast, due to their mild flavor.

## AFRICA AND ARABIA

Coffee Beans are grown on the continent of Africa, and the Middle East. The roast for this region's coffee beans should be dark to complement the balanced flavors that these beans possess.

The flavors are so varied they can have hints of chocolate or a spicy flavor. They can also have flavors that remind us of wine or citrus flavors as well. These coffees go great with both chocolate and cheese.

## INDONESIA AND THE PACIFIC ISLAND REGION

Coffee Beans from Asia and Indonesia have a lot of bodies, but not much acidity at all, these beans are earthy and hearty that should be used dark and very dark roast due to its robust flavors and to preserve its smooth and almost flowery undertones.

These beans are truly enjoyable with dark chocolate, caramel, and other rich desserts, but they are also delicious on their own.

## WHAT IS ACTUALLY IN A ROAST?

It is important to familiarize yourself with the different types of roasts and their characteristics. It is by far the fastest and easiest way to predict the flavor of the coffee beans you are about to brew. You do not only need to know the bean species and bean origin.

However, you also have to understand how the roast is mostly responsible for determining the aroma, body, and flavor of your chosen bean. Here are some simple tips to help you understand which brews do what things.

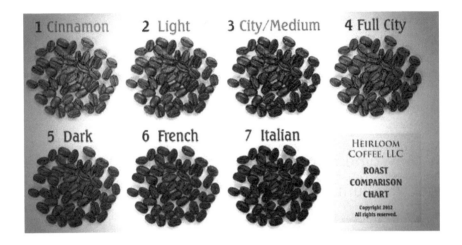

(Credit –Heirloom Coffee LLC)

1. Light Roasts have light brown butterscotch color. They have the least amount of body and acidity among all of these brews. Some also might say that they have the least amount of flavor as well. Which is true also, so be careful when choosing these type roast.

2. Medium Roasts have a chocolate brown color considerably more body and acidity than the light roasts, but less than other roasts.

3. Dark Roasts are a deep dark brown. This roast has the possibility to cause a reduction in flavor while increasing the body of the brew.

4. Dark roasts might seem like that produce a stronger cup; this is not the case. They actually produce a more consistent cup from start to finish.

5. Any type of bean from any region can be roasted light, medium, or dark.

When choosing a roast, your choice will depend on both the flavors of the coffee you prefer or want to offer and what kind of coffee you are brewing.

## TIPS FOR BUYING COFFEE BEANS

### Buy Local

Try to reduce the food miles involved in obtaining your coffee beans and products. Look to your local area for amazing coffee roasters. It might not be possible, but and asking around for local vendors can really help the environment and your local business area.

Helping other small business be successful helps you in turn by having a business in a booming location.

This also can be a great selling point. If you communicate with your customers, they might appreciate your shop even more.

When searching for a coffee supplier, do not be afraid to ask for samples. Coffee can only be judged by the taste in the cup. Don't make the mistake of buying something based on its branding or price. Choose your coffee based on the flavor, aroma, and anything else that think makes a good cup of coffee.

Many suppliers will be only too happy to either invite you to send some samples out to you. They know that tasting their coffee is what will get you to place an order if a coffee company refuses to give you samples when you ask, then it is time to strike them from your list.

One important advice I want to give you here, is any coffee sample you like for any suppliers, make sure to bring some with you and do a test brew with your own coffee maker this way you will know for sure how that coffee will taste in your store.

Coffee taste can vary widely based on the machine they are brewed with, due to the various water temperature of different machines.

Almost certainly when talking to suppliers, you will find a couple of new options for your menu that you had not previously thought of. Some smaller and more specialized suppliers might offer special single origin blends alongside their regular blends.

It could give you something unique over the competition. It is also always better to give your customers options by offering a larger coffee selection.

Talk to the experts and ask for their advice about the current trends in coffee and take this knowledge to make your coffee menu unique and innovative.

While you should not choose a coffee supplier based on the free things you can get, it is important to ask about additional services they can offer you as a customer. If they give free barista training, or ongoing support it makes your coffee purchase even better.

Here are some reputable food vendors that most restaurants in the US and Canada buy from.

- US Food
- Performance Food Group
- Food Services of America
- Shamrock Foods Company

There are hundreds of local food suppliers that you can find easily by doing Google search based on your location.

These vendors can supply you with everything you need from coffee to cake and even supplies like cups, straws, lid and paper plates and everything in-between.

My advice is to meet with every one of these companies and let them know your menu, let them decide what food and coffee they want to have you test.

They may invite you to their warehouse or to a food show where you will get to meet many other food vendors and will get to try each and every item that you would have on your menu. Once you like one of their items, time to negotiate the price and terms. Take your time to negotiate hard on both.

# BEST PRICING STRATEGY

## COMPETITIVE ANALYSIS

The key to any successful business is knowing what your bottom line is always. It is important to have a competitive analysis and know where your business stands within the retail coffee industry.

The competitive analysis allows you to get the information you need on your competitors, market share, market strategies, growth and other important factors. When you have all this information, you will be able to change or improve your business in key areas, so you can increase profits and sales.

Here is a simple way you can do a competitive analysis. On a piece of paper write down the following:

1. Number of local competitors you have
2. What is their niche/what type of coffees they sell
3. Where they sell
4. What is their pricing

Once you have that list, take a look and see where you would fit in that list, how can you stand out from the crowd, what can you do differently that would make customers pay attention to your products.

In my business experience, I believe there are three ways you can always stand above the crowd. I always have tried to stand above the crowd by trying of these three strategies.

1. By making superior products than my competitors make
2. By offering 100% customer satisfaction guarantee
3. By creative pricing strategy

Let me explain what I mean by creative pricing strategy.

## PRICING STRATEGY

Pricing is the most important factor in your business. A carefully thought out pricing strategy can make you very successful but a pricing strategy that places you above your market can literality put you out of business and on the other hand pricing below the market can wipe your bottom line profit completely clean, and before you know it, you are out of business and in debt.

That was the risky part; now the tricky part is if you stay with the market, then you are standing out in the crowd instead you are standing in the crowd.

In order to make yourself more visible and unique and to stand tall among other competitors, you have to be really very creative when it comes to your pricing strategy, and that is where the tricky part comes in.

My goal is to teach you how to implement a carefully thought out pricing strategy that can make you stand out and make you successful.

First, we want to discuss your buying price or the price you pay you to buy your inventory, because if you don't buy at the lowest possible price then you won't be able to sell them at a competitive price, nor you will be able to keep your margin. So, it is very vital that you negotiate hard and get the lowest possible price.

Now that you are buying your merchandise at a lowest possible price let's talk about the other half of this equation, the selling price and how much you should sell them for. When it comes to selling prices, this is where you have to be again very creative. Again, check your local area competitors and then decide where you need to be.

Remember the best pricing strategy is where you get to keep enough margin that makes your business profitable but at the same time you are not pricing yourself out of the market.

Coffee by far has one of the best margins compare to any other QSR (quick service restaurant). It is over 80% of gross profit which is huge by any standard.

Now let's discuss how we can calculate profit margin, markup and penny profit, so we all are on the same page.

## UNDERSTANDING PENNY PROFIT, PROFIT MARGIN, AND MARKUP

In business these are the three most common terms we hear every day, but what do they all mean and how they are different from each other, is a question many of you have.

Okay let's break them down and see what they are:

## PENNY PROFIT

Penny profit is essentially the actual cash profit you make by selling any items in your store. For example, say you just sold a bottle of 20 oz. Coke $1.75, what is the penny profit from that sale? To find the answer first, we need to see how much you paid to buy that bottle of Coke.

Looking at your invoice from Coke shows you paid $1.00 for that bottle of coke and you sold it for $1.75. So your penny profit is $1.75-1.00 = 75 cents. Penny profit is the difference between the selling price-actual costs.

## PROFIT MARGIN

Profit margin the term most widely used and understood in most every business as it is what we all use to figure out if we are making enough profit from our businesses by selling the products and services.

Profit margin is essentially the percentage of profit you make or earn when you sell a product. Confusing? Let's take a look at the same example of that bottle of coke we just used earlier.

We already know the penny profit from that sale was 75 cents. Now the profit margin is done little differently, to find out the exact margin we will have to take the penny profit and divide that number by the selling price. So it will be $1.75-$1.00=0.75, then we divide that penny profit by the selling price 0.75/$1.75 = 43% profit margin.

## MARKUP

The markup, on the other hand, is somewhat similar to profit margin, but instead of dividing the penny profit by the selling price you would have to divide the penny profit by the actual cost. Let's take a look at the same example once again.

Remember our penny profit from that bottle ok Coke? It was 75 cents; now we just need to divide that by the actual cost which was a $1.00 right? Let's do this, 0.75/$1.00 = 75% Markup for that same bottle of Coke.

Of course, the Markup has to take into consideration all of the factors we mentioned earlier, all of your associated costs needs to be included in your product. If you work out on average how many coffees' you will sell a day you can work out the average of your associated costs and find your breakeven point, then work towards your target sales.

Now after all your hard work, the setup is ready, the store is furnished, equipment in place, staff trained and ready to go. It's time for the test run. This is called a soft opening.

Invite your family, your accountant, your decorators, tradesmen, everyone from your area who you employed to help with the set up and of course, the family of your staff. This allows for your first bit of free advertising and promotion, and also, it's a great way to test run your premises.

It's at this stage you get to test run your staff, and everyone can get the feel for what it will be like. This is also a great time to fine tune anything that isn't working. Perhaps there is a leak under the sink, or one of the Coffee Machines won't heat up. The benefit of inviting those involved in the set-up is they may be on hand to attend to it, or to give more instruction and no one will be at all upset with this, as this is a pre-opening.

Make a list of anything you find that needs addressing, if there is a staff member struggling with nervousness, it's a good time to help them relax. Whatever issue you find, write it down, and find the solution right away.

Now is the time for planning the grand opening. Local radio stations and newspapers love this kind of thing as filler articles. You should invite them all along to your grand opening, and make sure to be available on this day to answer any questions, so overstaff if you have to.

Get those social media fingers going. Apps are even very easy to make these days and some outlets choose to have an app made where you can track purchases and give rewards. Word of mouth and asking friends and family to invite everyone they know is also a good start.

Always overstaff during the first few days or even the first week. That way you are going to be able to track your customer's movements and the area without finding yourself understaffed, leaving a bad taste in the mouths of your new customers.

Call ahead orders, cards that punch the 10$^{th}$ coffee free and competitions for a free coffee is always a great idea. Have a signature line of coffee, and even promotional items ready to hand out to people.

Call the local library and get a list of the book clubs. Many different clubs meet in Café's so be sure you have your specials and group discounts ready. You never know, you may just end up being the next go-to place for all those budding authors out there!

People love to offer their input. For the first week, when you hand your customers their order, ask them to fill in the short survey, where they can add drinks they would like to see, or any problems they can identify. Put them in a basket and do a lucky draw for a coffee. This serves as the start of a mailing list for events and functions, as well as involving your community in the process and development of your new business.

# MARKETING AND PROMOTION

The easiest way to gain new customers is by making your coffee shop seem appealing to people passing by. There is a growing trend of sign-less storefronts, but many shops still find them highly effective. It goes beyond just the letters hanging above the front door of your store.

Signage can help you brand your shop; it can help to direct traffic to your coffee shop. Directing customers to your shop is important. It does matter if your shop is on Main Street or on a street on the outskirts of town.

Samples are another way to draw people in. This method is used for foot traffic. If you have a tray of samples, it becomes so much easier to slow customers down and introduce them to the coffee shop and your products.

Keep in mind that First impressions really matter. For your coffee shop, the first impression is all about your storefront. So, decorate your store both inside and out. Use the tips in this book to create a cohesive them.

Every single customer that comes into your coffee shop is a marketing opportunity. That marketing opportunity is called word of mouth. When someone likes something, they tend to share that thing with the people they like and love.

Make your coffee shop the new thing that your customers are obsessed with. Also, people are most likely to trust the reviews of the people they know so a positive word of mouth review can go a long way.

While Social media is not a new marketing strategy anymore, it still is very effective one. Small business has a huge advantage with social media. Using these platforms to connect with people in your area can help your business feel like part of the community.

It is a free and easy way to publicize specials and events and show off people having a great time at your shop. You can also offer advice on making a great cup of coffee or share special recipes to connect with your customer base. Customers will respond to this positively and will tell others the really nice thing that you did for them.

Connecting with your surrounding community is essential to your success. Coffee shops rely heavily on the relationships they cultivate with their customers. Social media is a great start but being active online is just not enough. However, there are some great ways to ingrain yourself in the community.

One method is to sponsor an event close to everyone's heart. Weather that be a festival or a charity run or anything that brings an excited crowd. Showing your brand at these big town events help endear the people to you as well as helps you to gain additional customers.

Making sure that the community feels that you are with them, will make them want to be with you. These will be the customers that you will grow to rely on.

You can also, have in-house events such as coffee tastings or live bands. Getting customers in your shop, and having a good time is a great way to connect with future customers.

If you put on events that everyone is excited about, then you have helped to make yourself a destination for the community. If they come for an event, they just might come back for a cup of coffee the next day.

Customer Reviews are importantly similar to word of mouth people like to hear reviews from other real people, even if they do not know those people. That means the better reviews you have online, the better your business will most likely do. There are several things you can do to obtain positive reviews.

The first thing is always to have a great product line and great customer service. You cannot have positive reviews of customers who don't have positive experiences. The easiest way to get reviews on sites like Yelp is to ask your customers directly. After filling a customer's order, ask that customer to rate their experience on a website like Yelp. A simple reminder will result in more reviews from people who might not have thought to do so.

You can also place a sign near the cash register or have that be the home screen of Yelp when anyone logs in to the free Wi-Fi. Encouraging people to posit reviews. If these reminders aren't doing enough to get you a satisfactory amount of reviews, try offering a discount to anyone who provides a screenshot of the review they made.

Emphasize that even if it is a negative review, they will still receive the discount, and you will do whatever needs to be done to make their experiences better in the future.

When considering marketing, graphic design is one of the first things that should come to mind. With the help of a great graphic designer, you will be able to make a cohesive visual marketing strategy.

The first thing you have to do is find a graphic designer you work well with. In order to find the best graphic designer for you, you need to consider your wants and needs. If you're in the market for small jobs, your best bet is sites like Fiverr.com or for bigger jobs 99designs.com.

These online talent platforms gather many graphic designers from all around the world. You can either post your job and let talents bid on them, or you can look through various profiles and read their reviews then hire someone directly.

It is best to describe your job requirements in detail, let's assume you want a new logo. The first thing you want to do is write down all your needs, color choices and provide some logo designs you like from other companies. Don't worry, you are not trying to copy from other companies, just showing them what type of logos' you want.

You also would say the scalability you want for the logo. If you want a logo for business cards and coffees, you should say so here, even if that means you have to have different but very similar logos for different sizes.

Remember to make sure that your logo makes sense in grayscale, and for those that are red-green colorblind. At the end of your description, you want to detail the price that you feel is fair for your project.

You can get a logo done at Fiverr.com for $5, but it may not be what you want or suitable to your liking, the next best option is 99designs.com. This site is little more expensive but well worth it.

You can also use more general classifieds like Craigslist, in your area, or freelancer websites like Upwork.com, freelancer.com and guru.com that connect you with many types of a freelancer. Using many of methods can create a large of candidates you'll have to look through. That means you will need to be rigorous with your choosing process, described next.

So, after you've messaged several candidates, you now have to choose just one graphic designer, unlike other jobs, rely on portfolios instead of resumes.

Make sure that you consider whether you like their prior work.

Designers will not change their style to match yours; they never deviate from their own chosen style. You cannot force them to see your vision, instead, take some time to find the kind of person whose vision matches your own. That is where you would really succeed.

The next thing you want to do is call their references. However, don't get excited when their references are positive.  They wouldn't be listed as references, otherwise

Instead, you're looking for amazing recommendations. Things that go beyond saying they are good to work with. You want to hear how amazing this graphic designer is, how they wouldn't work for anyone else. Most importantly they need to rave about them always delivering on time and budget.

Once you are fully satisfied, go ahead and hire the designer of your choice.

Make sure to get things in writing, so there's no confusion when it comes time for payment.

The contract should state that you get all of the electronic source files of all works, this is important so that you can make any small changes by yourself or switch to an entirely different designer.

The very last thing that needs to be found before you're ready to put your graphic designer to work is to get to know each other. You want to figure out how to work together.

The designer will want things like a clear direction, so give them that direction. If you are unsure, bring that confusion to the table and work with your graphic designer and come up with a solution. Don't let your graphic designer muddy your vision, but also don't be so confusing to the point where no one even knows your vision.

Just take things one step at a time when it comes to the design work. Instead of making a grand plan for everything, start small. For example, just focus on choosing the best color scheme and an interesting logo first.

After you get the basics totally finished and approved. You will have a much easier time getting the rest to fall into place. Once your colors, attitude, and style are embodied in something as iconic as a logo, the path to websites, white papers, blogs, and tradeshow banners becomes an extension of an idea rather than a new project.

Finally, "baby-steps" means you can spend only what you want. If you end up not liking to work with each other or what you want ends up being too expensive, you can stop and still have something to show for it for your next designer, or maybe you can try to do the rest yourself.

## 5 CREATIVE PROMOTION FOR YOUR NEW COFFEE HOUSE

### Here Are Some Great Specials You Can Offer

• "Coffee of the Month Club": Offer a discount on a new type of coffee every month. This can add excitement to your offers and keep people coming for just one type of discounted coffee

• BOGOs: Having a "buy one get one free" promotion every few months can really boost a low selling item. It also seems to be an incredible deal that just calls for people to take advantage of.

• Don't ever try just low balling your competitors with your price point. This will only lead to frustration and less profit in the long run. Remember, you have to maintain a price point where you can profit and grow your business.

• Holiday Promotions: You can run different packages during the holidays. Examples of these can be festive packages or packets with coffee bags accessories, and other items with your logo on it.

• It is important to remember that when it comes to pricing or marketing strategies, there is no option that will work for everyone. Some strategies may work better for you than others.

Some ideas will work now, but not be such a great fit later. So, it is important to test each idea separately and then make sure to document the results and see which one worked the best.

## FIGURE OUT WHAT YOUR COMPETITORS OFFER, THEN MAKE IT BETTER

If a coffee shop has a unique offering, figure out what it is, and how you can come up with a product that would overshadow theirs. If they offer a large number of flavors in their drinks, see what they don't have, and push that. Find a different angle and then promote it like crazy.

## OFFER A FULL CUSTOMER SATISFACTION GUARANTEE

Having a guarantee of service is a great way to show customers that you stand behind what you create. It also indicates that you will always put the customer and their individual needs and experiences first in your business.

This is an important message to send that would encourage people to give you a try for the first time.

# LAST WORDS

In this book, I have gone through the steps of successfully opening a coffee shop business. After reading this book, if you do decide to open such a store then it is time for you to come up with a solid and precise business plan as I discussed at the beginning of the book.

No, I am not asking you to write a 50-page business plan but a plan that outlines where you will get the funding, what you want in your coffee shop, and what area of the city you want this business to be and in what time frame do you want to accomplish this goal. A plan where you figure out in which directions you

Remember you only get one chance to make a great first impression, so when planning, make sure you add some "wow" factors, this way you will make a great first impression. To make such impression, you don't need to spend extra money, but you have to be creative and figure out what makes customers go wow.

Keep your focus on the quality and marketing side of your business, and you will see success sooner rather than later.

Hopefully, in this book, I was able to give you a good general overview of starting a trendy coffee shop business. Now get out there and start figuring out you can make this dream a reality. And be successful. Remember, we only live once, so why not try to be the best you can be and see where that may take you.

I wanted to thank you for buying my book; I am not a professional writer or author, but rather a person who always had the passion for starting various food-related businesses. In this book I wanted to share my knowledge with you, as I know there are many people who share the same passion and drive as I do. So, this book is fully dedicated to YOU, my readers.

Despite my best effort to make this book error free, if you happen to find any mistakes, I want to ask for your forgiveness.

Just remember, my writing skills may not be best, but the knowledge I share here is pure and honest.

If you thought I added some value and shared some valuable information that you can use, please take a minute and post a review on wherever you bought this book from. I read every review I get, and if you leave your contact information, I will personally email you to say "Thanks." This will mean the world to me. Thank you so much!!

Lastly, I wanted to thank my wife Rebecca and my daughter Marisa for all their help and support throughout this book, without them, this book would not have been possible.

Once again, thank you from the bottom of my heart for reading this book, I wish you all the best of luck and great success and happiness in life.

# HELPFUL RESOURCES

https://coffeebi.com/#

https://coffeeshopstartups.com/

https://www.sba.gov/

http://www.ncausa.org

http://Wikipedia.org

https://www.irs.gov/businesses/small-businesses-self-employed/how-to-apply-for-an-ein

http://zesco.com

## FOR BUSINESS PLAN

http://BPlans.com

## FOR POS SYSTEM

https://www.shopkeep.com/business-types/coffee-shop-pos

https://squareup.com/pos/coffee-shop

https://coffeeshopstartups.com/best-coffee-shop-pos-system/

# FOR RESTAURANT EQUIPMENT

http://www.ncausa.org

http://www.ebay.com/bhp/used-restaurant-equipment

https://www.acitydiscount.com/

http://kescoflorida.com/

https://www.webstaurantstore.com/restaurant-equipment.html

http://Bunn.com

# FOR EMPLOYEE TRAINING

http://www.itsimulations.com/training-courses/online-restaurant-training/

http://www.restauranttraininguniversity.com/

http://servicethatsells.com/online-restaurant-training/

https://www.restaurantowner.com/public/Restaurant-Training-Manual-Templates.cfm

http://www.jeansrestaurantsupply.com/restaurant-equipment/used-restaurant-equipment.html